May 11, 2014

Welcome to the
Lord's table!

Many blessings for
years to come — Love,
The Willetts

GLORIA
Children's Books

Nihil Obstat, Arthur J. Scanlan, S.T.D., Censor Liborum
Imprimatur ✠ Francis Cardinal Spellman,
Archbishop of New York
Cum Permissu Superiorum

William J. Hirten Co., Cumberland, RI

GLORIA
Children's Books

Favorite Prayers
For Catholic Children

by Daniel A. Lord, S.J.

Before You Begin To Pray

Before you start to pray, always remember:
That you are God's child.
That He is very close to you.
He can hear all that you say.
He will give you what you ask for,
if it is good for you.
He loves you very much.
When you pray, you are just talking to God.
And God is the One who loves you most.
So prayer is easy. It is just talking
things over with God
God is waiting to hear you when you pray.
Talk to Him from your heart.

The Sign Of The Cross

Catholics begin their day, their prayer,
and their activiaties
with the Sign of the Cross.
The Sign of the Cross strengthens us
in temptations and difficulties
and reminds us of Jesus' love for us.

**In the name of the Father,
and of the Son,
and of the Holy Spirit.
Amen.**

God is my Father. He made my body and my soul. He gave me everything good. He wants me to come to Him some day in Heaven.

The Our Father

Our Father Who art in Heaven
Hallowed be Thy name.
Thy Kingdom come,
Thy will be done
on earth at it is in Heaven.
Give us this day, our daily bread
and forgive us our tresspasses as we forgive
those who trespass against us.
Lead us not into temptation
but deliver us from evil.
Amen.

9

I honor and thank Jesus, the Son of God,
Who came to save us all from sin.

... My Jesus, Mercy!
... Sacred Heart of Jesus. I trust in You.
... Dear Jesus, I love you.
... Dear Jesus help me to do as I am told.
Bless my father and my mother.
Bless all those I love.
... Dear Jesus, You loved Your dear Mother so.
You did what she told You.
Help me to be good to my mother.
... Dear Infant Jesus, never let me make You
sad by my sins.
... Jesus, when I have to do hard things,
help me to do them at once.
... Dear Jesus, I am so glad that You love me.
Put Your kind hands on me and bless me.
Keep me safe from harm.
Amen.

The Holy Spirit is the third Person
of the Blessed Trinity.
He is a divine Person and He is God.
He is also our Friend.
He wants to give us His many gifts,
blessings, graces and virtues.
Jesus gave us the Holy Spirit to help us live
in His love and in truth.

Prayer To The Holy Spirit

Come Holy Spirit, fill the hearts of
Your faithful and enkindle
in them the fire of Your love.
Send forth Your Spirit and they shall be created
and You shall renew the face of the earth.
Amen.

13

The Glory Be

Another important prayer is this
prayer to God.
God is One divine Being in Three Persons,
and He has existed forever.
I should speak to Each Person of God
as my Friend.
In this prayer, I praise and thank the
Trinity for making the world.
I also look forward to being
with God forever in Heaven,
where I will be someday if I love Him.
**Glory be to the Father, and to the Son,
and to the Holy Spirit.
As it was in the begining, is now,
and ever shall be, world without end.
Amen.**

14

Then you offer God the whole day.
When you do this, the day becomes very
important. God is happy.
He is pleased that you give Him your day.
He blesses you.
Everything you do
will make you happier in Heaven.

O, dear Father...
I offer You my day...
Everything I do today, I will do for You...
Please accept me as Your child...
Please take my day as my gift to You...
I want to spend it as Your Son Jesus did...
I want to act like Mary Your Mother did...
I want to make others around me happy...
Help me to spend it well...
Through Christ Our Lord. Amen.

Then I honor our
dear Mother in Heaven;
Mary, who is Jesus' Mother also.

The Hail Mary

Hail Mary full of grace
the Lord is with you.
Blessed art thou amongst women
and blessed is the fruit
of thy womb Jesus.
Holy Mary, Mother of God,
pray for us sinners
now and at the hour of our death.
Amen.

Then I talk to Jesus, Mary and Joseph.
This is the Holy Family.

Jesus, Mary and Joseph...
I offer you my heart and my soul...
Jesus, Mary and Joseph...
Please help me when I need your help...
Jesus, Mary and Joseph...
I give you my soul to keep in peace.
Jesus, Mary and Joseph...
Keep my family safe and happy.
Amen.

On Sundays and Holy Days,
we pray the **Apostles' Creed**.
This is a great Act of Faith.
It was written a long time ago.
It shows that we know the truth.
It says that we have listened to Jesus Christ.
It means that we believe in His Church.

I believe in God, the Father almighty,
Creator of heaven and earth,
and in Jesus Christ, his only Son, our Lord,
who was conceived by the Holy Spirit,
born of the Virgin Mary,
suffered under Pontius Pilate,
was crucified, died and was buried;
he descended into hell;
on the third day he rose again from the dead;
he ascended into heaven,
and is seated at the right hand
of God the Father almighty;
from there he will come to judge
the living and the dead.
I believe in the Holy Spirit,
the holy catholic Church,
the communion of saints,
the forgiveness of sins,
the resurrection of the body,
and life everlasting. Amen.

23

Then you ask your Guardian Angel
to take care of you.
When you were born,
God gave you an Angel for a friend.
He is always with you.
He protects you from harm.
He watches over you when you sleep.
He is a dear friend.
He likes you to talk to him.

O, Angel of God...
My Guardian dear...
To whom God's love...
Commits me here...
Ever this day...
Be at my side...
To light, to guard...
To rule and guide.
Amen.

What happens when you pray?
Well, God listens and smiles and says,
"I'll take care of you, My child."
Maybe you can't hear Him.
That isn't necessary.
Right away, He is near you.
He helps you to be good.
He drives away evil things
and evil people who might hurt you.
He says, "My child is good, and loves Me;
I will make him/her happy."
When you ask for things that are good for you,
He gives them to you.
He helps you grow to be a strong child.
He brings you safely through life,
so you will grow up to be
good Catholic adults.